HOW TO CARE FOR YOUR CAT

The Complete Guide from Kitten to Adult

By Catcare Specialists

Table of Contents

Introduction

In this book, you'll find everything you need to know about how to properly care for, train, feed, vaccinate and raise your feline friend into the perfect little walking, talking and stalking ball of fur. It is the essential guide which covers everything you need to know. From advice on feeding, training and keeping them entertained, to staying on top of their vaccinations and correcting bad behaviors. It is our job to help you understand your feline and help you give him or her the best home you can provide. The decision to adopt your first kitten or cat is a monumental one for both you and for the cat. He will be one of the family. Whether you are thinking about getting a cat or you have adopted or bought one and you want to know to best take care of it, or even if you have adopted or bought one and are starting to panic about what you should be doing, then this book has been designed for you to make your relationship with this special kitten or cat a lasting one.

We will cover everything you need to know throughout the cat's lifecycle and talk about things such as behavioural problems in cats, such as avoiding the litter box, excessive meowing and other attention-seeking or destructive behaviors. These types of behaviors are easier to stop early on but even if you have adopted an older cat it can be corrected by identifying the problem, then initiating a program of gradual retraining. Remember that there are no bad cats, only uninformed owners.

You can keep this book as a guide or user manual throughout your cat's life as it covers all the areas you need to know so keep it handy on the book shelf. We believe that cats make for great pets and can be easier to maintain than some other common pets such as dogs which require more upkeep. It's exciting having a pet and we hope through this book that you can give your kitten or cat the love and care that all animals deserve.

Bringing Your Kitten Home

Moving to a new home is stressful for a kitten. Give it plenty of reassurance and time to adjust to new surroundings before making introductions to other animals or people in the household. Ensure that all doors and windows are closed and a guard is in front of the fireplace if you have one. Kittens are small and agile and like to explore every area of the house. Make sure the kitten knows where the bed, litter box and food/water bowls are, this is important and should be done as soon as possible.

The kitten's bed should be a safe place to go when things get too much to handle, it is like the pillow forts of the kitten world. You never want kittens to feel anxious or threatened so put the bed somewhere out of the way preferably or tucked into a corner. The bed needs to be in a warm, dry comfortable place that is easily accessible for the kitten. Buy a bed from a pet shop or use a strong, dry, cardboard box with a hole cut in the side and some blankets inside. It should contain soft bedding preferably as it is comparable to snuggling into the mother or it's brother and sister kittens which gives them a sense of serenity. On the first few nights a warm water bottle (not hot) under a blanket may help compensate for the absence of the kitten's mother or litter-mates. If you happen to have, or can borrow, a large secure pen, this is ideal for providing a safe den and can hold the kitten's litter tray and bed and is an excellent way to keep them safe before introducing other animals, though we know a pen isn't always a viable option for people. The trick is to slowly introduce them to their new world.

Introduction to household residents should be gradual, gentle and quiet if possible. Children must be taught that the newcomer is not a toy and they should be patient and not pick up the kitten but sit on the floor and wait for the animal to come to them or gently bring them over to the kids when the kids are calm and ready. Playing stops when the kitten chooses and the kitten should be allowed to go back to bed undisturbed as we all need a pillow fort to hide in when things get stressful. The children should be aware that the kitten may scratch and play-bite and that they should not rile them as this might encourage the kitten to become aggressive or they might learn it is an acceptable way to behave.

Introducing a kitten to a dog or cat needs to be done carefully. An ideal way is to have a large mesh pen, in which the kitten can sit safely while the cat or dog becomes accustomed to the new presence. Particular care should be taken with introductions to some dogs. Those not used to cats need to be kept as calm as possible, on a lead, and told to sit quietly. Let the dog sniff the kitten when the dog is calm as this is how dogs communicate and learn about new animals. Make sure the dog is calm and relaxed and pet and reassure the dog calmly as well. Keeping the kitten in the pen, while the dog sits outside of it is best as it allows the kitten to take its time in the approach – eventually the pen can be removed to allow both animals to physically interact. This can happen gradually over some time and requires patience and rewards for the dog for behaving well.

For quieter dogs, or those used to cats, introductions can be made using a strong cat carrier. Keep the dog on a lead initially, placing the carrier on a high surface and allowing controlled introductions short and frequently. Most dogs soon calm down when they realize the newcomer is not particularly interesting and you can progress to direct meetings with the dog, on a lead initially for safety. Do not leave the new pet alone with dogs or cats until your kitten is well established in the household. If you don't have the pen or carrier then carry the kitten gently and make sure to be ready to pull the kitten away if the dog gets too excited as they may get carried away and playfully lick or nibble the kitten. Slow, calm, patient and frequent introductions is the key.

Socialization is important for your kitten to live confidently and safely in your household. The optimum time for kitten socialization is between two and seven weeks so before choosing your kitten or cat, find out what experiences your kitten has had with other animals, if any. A kitten raised in a home or adoption center where staff are aware of the importance of socialization should cope well with the move to a new family. However, litters born and raised outdoors, and kittens from feral litters, may not have enough experience with humans to adapt fully to a family or may take vastly longer to adjust.

Bottle Milk and Nutrition for Kittens

If you're responsible for taking care of kittens in the first few months of their lives you need to know what milk to use and how often to feed them. Kittens will drink milk from weeks zero to week four, then they will slowly transition from milk to solid kitten food at around five to eight weeks. So, in total, you will bottle feed them for eight weeks. This process of moving them to solid food is known as weaning, which we will cover in the next chapter. Kittens that are still with their mother are easier to take care of as the mother will milk them until she cannot produce any more milk and then she will naturally and gradually stop them from breast feeding and offer them other sources of food, which in the wild would be small animals such as mice, but for domesticated cats then they will transition to solid food. Unless you want to start hunting small mice yourself in the middle of the night for your domesticated cat, I would suggest the transition to formulated kitten food or gruel, which is soft or mushy semi-solid food.

What are the kittens' milk requirements for the first four weeks?

- If you own the newborn kitten and its mother is there you should have nothing to worry about when it comes to feeding them. Their mother's milk provides 100 percent of the nutritional needs and you don't have to give them cat food until after the first four weeks of life.

- If the mother cat becomes sick, cannot produce enough milk, or the kittens are found as orphans, you may use a milk replacement.

- When feeding the kitten for the first time, up to two weeks, hold the syringe or teat close to the kitten's mouth and she will instinctively start feeding.

- NEVER feed the kitten on her back or with her head held high, her posture is very important and she should be resting or lying belly down with the bottle or syringe straight in front of her. Having her head tilted too high can cause aspiration which is the inhalation of the formula into the lungs, which can be highly damaging and even fatal.

- During the first weeks of life a kitten's body weight may double or even triple. This rapid growth will continue, albeit at a decreasing rate, until maturity. Copious amounts of energy and nutrients are required in balanced quantities to support this spectacular growth spirt so feed the kitten often.

- Kittens both need and use copious amounts of energy as you are probably aware from the fact that they start to not sit still and start chasing things and trying to climb everything in sight. They need energy about two to three times that of an adult cat which they will get from their formulated milk. Kittens also need about 30 percent of their total energy from protein. Make sure the milk you offer is specifically formulated for kittens. Regular milk isn't catered towards your kitten's high energy needs and may not sit well in your kitty's stomach and cause diarrhea. Your pet will need to eat kitten-formula milk until she reaches maturity.

- Formulated milk and bottles can be bought from pet stores, vets or online and they all have information on how to use them and what ages of the kitten they are suitable for. Milk replacement or formulated milk comes in tubs or drums and is a dry powder or liquid. Follow the instructions on the packet on how many scoops to use and how much water to mix if needed. Kittens need warm milk so there will be instructions on how to heat the milk, usually placing the bottle in hot or warm water. Make sure the milk is lukewarm or body temperature and not hot before feeding. The amount of milk to feed the kitten per day should be on the instructions of the formulated milk.

- Make sure the kitten is warm when they are feeding. You can wrap her up in a small towel or blanket and make sure you are sitting comfortably yourself as you will have to be patient while your little furball feeds.

Weaning Your Cat

What Is Weaning?

Weaning is the process of transitioning kittens from mother's milk/formulated milk to solid food. During weaning the kittens gradually progress from dependence on a mother's care to social independence. Think of it as the early teenage years of the kitten world minus the pimples. The kittens will start to gain their independence and want to take on the world by themselves and their behaviors and personalities will start to become more apparent. Ideally, weaning is handled entirely by the mother cat. However, if the kittens in your care have been separated from their mother or if you are fostering a litter or you have a pregnant cat about to give birth and you are seeing the young ones through to a successful weaning process, then this information will be important.

What Age Should Kittens Be Weaned?

The weaning process normally begins when kittens are around four weeks old, and is usually completed when they reach eight to ten weeks. If you oversee weaning an orphaned kitten, please remember that weaning should not be attempted at too early of an age. Generally, when a kitten's eyes are open and able to focus, and he/she is steady on his/her feet, the introduction of solid food can safely begin which is usually around four to five weeks.

How Long Does It Take to Wean a Kitten?

The process typically takes between four and six weeks, with most kittens completely weaned by the time they're eight to ten weeks old.

How Do I Start the Weaning Process?

It's important to remember that abrupt removal from the mother cat can have a negative effect on the kittens' health and socialization skills. They learn to eat, use a litter box and play, among other things, by observing their mother. Whenever possible, kittens should remain with their mother during the weaning process, as she will inherently know what to do. When the kittens reach four weeks old, you can place them in a separate area for a few hours at a time to reduce their dependency on mother's milk and her overall presence. Put them in their own specific area with a litter box and food and water bowls. As the kittens become more independent, they can spend more time away from their mother until they are completely weaned. Encourage them when separated from their mother to eat the solid food and use formulated kitten food or soak the solid food in milk to soften it. Serve kitten milk replacement in a shallow bowl. Do not use cow's milk, as this will cause stomach upset and diarrhea in some kittens. Dip your fingertip (or the syringe or bottle the kitten is used to nursing from) into the liquid, let the kitten lick it, then guide him by moving your finger down into the bowl. Please do not push his nose into the bowl. He may inhale the liquid and develop pneumonia or other lung problems. Once he/she becomes accustomed to lapping liquids, create a gruel as described below. Though you should continue to bottle-feed while the kitten is learning to eat from the bowl, you can help with the gradual transition by always offering the bowl first, and then the bottle.

How Do I Transition the Kitten to Solid Food?

Make a gruel by mixing a high-quality dry or canned kitten food with kitten milk replacement until it is the consistency of oatmeal. As the kitten gets accustomed to eating, gradually decrease the amount of milk replacement you add, while slowly increasing the amount of kitten food. By five to six weeks, he should be eating only lightly moistened food. Now you can start to leave out lesser amounts of dry food and fresh water always. By eight to 10 weeks, kittens should be accustomed to eating dry kitten food.

What About Weaning an Orphaned Kitten?

Generally, orphaned or hand-fed kittens can begin weaning slightly earlier, at about three weeks of age, but otherwise the process is essentially the same. Begin by offering milk replacement in a dish, teaching the kitten how to lap from the dish. Gradually transition to a gruel created by mixing a commercial milk replacement with high-quality kitten food. As the kitten slowly grows accustomed to eating, gradually reduce the amount of milk replacement you use. By five to six weeks of age, he should be relying solely on kitten food for his nutrients so you can put the bottle away now.

What Are Some Tips to Help the Weaning Process?

Kittens may play with the gruel, batting it around and stepping into the bowl before they understand that it's food. Have patience and don't rush the process, they'll catch on eventually. In the meantime, use a soft, moist cloth to wipe any formula off the animal's face and feet after each feeding. Gently dry him/her with a towel and keep him in a warm area free of drafts until he's completely dry.

Beyond the Litter Box

Unfortunately, cats don't always connect with the litter box. Even cats that know the drill will sometimes choose another spot at home. "House-soiling" can become a concern for even the best cat owners. It can be a sign of a serious health issue or simply the result of changes around the house so if it persists for a long time then consider seeing a veterinarian as there might be a health issue. In the majority of cases, paying close attention to clues will allow you to deal with the situation before it arises or put a premature end to a potentially unwanted problem. So, what do we look out for?

Signs of a House-Soiling problem would include the following:

- A consistent pattern of urinating and/or defecating outside the litter box

- Urine spraying which would be urine marks around doorways, windows or new objects in the house

- Spending longer than a normal amount of time in the litter box

- Vocalizing while in the litter box

- Going to the litter box more often than normal

Potential causes of House-Soiling:

- Health issues ranging from diabetes mellitus to lower urinary tract disease

- A dirty litter box or inadequate number of litter boxes in the home. There should be at least one box per kitten/cat but an extra one is recommended, especially in bigger houses. If you have multiple boxes the litter boxes need to be in various locations in the house, not all in one room.

- Litter box is in a remote, noisy or unpleasant surrounding

- Litter box is inappropriate. Covered boxes can maintain odors and large cats may not be able to move around enough in small boxes

- Wrong type of litter or sudden change in litter type

- Social changes such as the addition of a new cat or the sudden presence of outdoor cats

- Infrequent changing of litter box

- Infrequent routines or travelling a lot

- Having multiple cats

If you experience house-soiling then consider adjusting based on some of the factors described above. If the problem continues over a prolonged period, consult your veterinarian to investigate possible health problems. Multiple cats require multiple litter boxes, one for each of the cats. The litter box should be at least 1½ times the length of your cat and once placed shouldn't be moved to various locations. Please note that not all cats like litter box covers or liners. Make sure the litter box is in an easy-to-find, quiet place away from high-traffic areas of the house where other pets or people won't likely disrupt your cat's routine. Think pillow fort. Somewhere quiet and peaceful where he will not be disturbed. Place the boxes in various locations in the house, not in the same room. Fill your cat's litter box with about an inch-and-a-half of natural clay or clumping litter. Although clay and clumping litters are preferred by cats, some cats prefer different litter textures. If your cat will not use clay or clumping litter, try different litters until you find one your cat prefers.

Scoop twice daily and change litter completely every week because your cat will prefer to use a clean litter box. Consider feeding a cat food that reduces stool odor. Always wash the box with a mild detergent before refilling it with litter. Never touch or disrupt your cat while using the litter box. Contact your veterinarian if your cat goes to the bathroom outside the litter box, stays in the litter box longer than normal, or vocalizes while in the box because a medical problem might be the cause.

Vaccinations

Routine vaccination has greatly reduced the extent of several feline diseases (including some that can prove fatal). It is vital that your cat has all the necessary vaccinations and boosters. Please consult your local vet for more information on vaccinations.

What vaccines does my cat need?

- **Feline infectious enteritis (FIE) - *a vaccination must***

Feline infectious enteritis (a severe and often fatal gut infection) is caused by the feline parvovirus (or feline panleukopenia virus). Vaccination against FIE has been very successful. Unvaccinated cats are at significant risk because the virus is widespread in the environment.

- ***Cat 'flu*** - *a vaccination must*

Two types of cat 'flu are vaccinated against feline herpesvirus (FHV-1) and feline calicivirus (FCV). These viruses are very common and vaccination will protect your cat against prolonged illness, but because there are many different strains of cat 'flu the vaccine will not totally eradicate the threat.

- **Feline leukaemia virus (FeLV)** - *a vaccination must for outdoor cats*

FeLV is a lifelong infection and unfortunately most cats will die within three years of diagnosis, usually from a subsequent disease like leukaemia, lymphoma (tumors) or progressive anaemia. It is not an airborne disease and can only be passed on via direct contact between cats (usually by saliva or bites). Because of the serious nature of the disease, CP recommends FeLV vaccination.

- **Feline chlamydophilosis** - *depends on your circumstances*

This bacterium, which causes conjunctivitis in cats, can't survive in the atmosphere and is thus spread by direct contact between cats (affecting multi-cat households and kittens predominantly). Your vet will discuss your situation and advise as to whether this vaccine is necessary.

Your Cats First Month at Home

If you have just bought or adopted an adult cat, moved to a new house or even just borrowed your friends cat while they are on holiday, then your cat will likely take a few days to settle into the unfamiliar environment. If it's the former, you can start thinking about long-term care and making sure you're prepared for a long, happy life together. Here are some basics to get you started in the first month.

Bedding: Just like with the kittens you need to get the right kind of bed for your cat to sleep in. Cats can sleep up to 18 hours a day, so creating the right conditions for your new cat is important. Make sure bedding is soft and washable, and place it inside a basket, small box, cozy corner or a particularly ideal sunny spot of the house.

Sleeping: Beware of letting your cat sleep with you. Remember that cats tend to be nocturnal which may disrupt your sleep and if you know any cat owners, they will tell you that they almost always disturb your sleep if they aren't trained properly. Early morning scratching and jumping about and even meowing isn't a good thing to be woken up to every morning. If you want to train the cat to sleep in your bed or room then train them early and if late night antics wake you up, gently put your cat on the floor. Don't reward a disruption with attention or you're inviting your cat to wake you up over and over.

Travelling or transporting: Keeping your cat safe when travelling to your new home. Cat carriers are the safest, most comfortable way to travel. Before hitting the road, take time to familiarize your cat with the carrier by storing toys in it or making it a cozy place for a nap inside your home. Good toys for cats are easy to find and widely available at pet stores so make sure he/she has some favorite toys and try and get him used to the toys if possible before putting them in the carrier.

Proper identification and collars: Always have an ID tag and proper registration information attached to your cat's collar (rabies, license, etc.). A collar should fit with some slack but not so loose that it slips over your cat's head. Allow two finger-widths of space between the neck and collar. If your cat is an outdoor cat you can get printed tags with your address or mobile number made in case of emergencies.

Indoor vs Outdoor Cat

Most owners allow their cats the freedom of the great outdoors to do whatever it is that cats do all day outside, and then care, feed and enjoy social interaction with them when they return home. Only about 10% of cats are believed to live permanently indoors in the UK, although the figure is increasing and is already much higher in the USA, where keeping cats indoors is encouraged. Indoor cats are getting more common in the cities for example, where owners live in apartments or where it may be too dangerous for the cat to roam about on busy roads and streets and pet owners naturally become more concerned for their safety.

Until fairly recently all cats spent part of their day outside hunting, patrolling their territory and relieving themselves. It wasn't until the invention of cat litters in the 1950s that cat owners had a choice over which type of cat they wanted to raise. Some pet owners then began to keep cats indoors for their own safety. Indeed, indoor cats can live longer and have physically healthier lives than cats allowed outdoors but on the down side, indoor cats are also more likely to suffer psychological problems and develop behavioral problems when compared to their outdoor neighbors.

There is a small risk that cats with outdoor access will move home for one reason or another, get lost or accidentally shut away in sheds and garages. There is also a small risk they may get taken in by someone else or are passed on as strays to homing organizations to be found new homes (which is why it is important to have them tagged and have collars with identification).

Sadly, one in four cats will perish under the wheels of a car in the UK, with death on the roads being highest in the first year of life. If a cat survives its first year and learns about dangers in his environment, its chances to live a long life are significantly increased. A cat in the city is thought to be at even greater risk from being injured or killed on the road than one in suburbia or the countryside, simply because of the greater volume of traffic and numbers of roads, but many cats in the countryside also fall prey to cars. The unexpected lone vehicle passing down a lonely road can often catch out the relaxed and unwary cat, and for that reason some owners in rural areas also choose to keep their pet indoors for safety reasons. Young cats in rural areas may also be at risk from wild predators or poison left by baits for countryside vermin.

Indoor cats are unlikely to catch diseases that cats can pass to one another, are protected against injuries and resulting infections that might arise from fighting, and are far less likely to contract parasites, such as fleas and worms. Some timid and older cats may also prefer to stay indoors anyway because it is warm, well protected and away from all the startling and scary things outside.

There is no doubt that indoor cats live longer and safer lives than cats allowed to hunt and explore outdoors, but what of their mental welfare? The cat began to evolve 13 million years ago and ultimately became a top-of-the-food-chain predator and solitary hunter. This means that a cat has evolved to move through its hunting environment avoiding danger and stalking its prey. To do this, cats have developed astonishing sensory powers like super heroes. They have specialized eyesight that functions at low light levels when their common prey such as rodents are most active and when birds are roosting. They have a sense of hearing that extends way up into the range employed by bats so that they can hear the very high frequency chattering of rats or mice. Their sense of smell, although largely reserved for social organization rather than hunting, is also far superior to ours, and that of most dogs. Along with their very touch sensitive whiskers and guard hairs, cats can be regarded as super-sensory compared with social hunter-gatherers like man, or hunter-scavengers like dogs, that find much of their food as part of a team and can rely on one another to detect and respond to danger.

Many people feel that a cat should be able to go outside if it needs to and if it can. There's a huge part of a cat's life that we're unaware of, where it uses all its highly evolved senses and talents. It can hunt, patrol its territory, mark, sunbathe and generally indulge all the behaviors it is naturally programmed to use. Inside our homes the cat is really a shadow of its potential self, with its engine and navigation system and weapons switched off. It is like a superhero on a desert island with no arch enemy to fight to save the world. Outside the desert island, Superfeline comes to life and sharpens up its talents and its body by hunting, climbing and exploring.

Given that a cat which must hunt to feed itself would need to eat at least ten mice a day, and that each actual catch might require three hunts, you can see that a 'normal' cat would spend a lot of its day actively seeking food. It would also need to make sure that its coat is clean and well-groomed so that it's sensitive, waterproof and doesn't carry a heavy smell that might give it away. That dedication to achieving a perfect coat takes a long time, and for the rest of the time the cat probably sleeps. Thus, an active normal cat won't sleep all the time in the same way as it's able to do when stuck at home and given everything it needs.

Weighing up the pros and cons will help you decide what is best for your cat. It is easier to have an indoor only cat right from the start than to convert an outdoor cat successfully into an indoor one. The benefits of keeping the cat away from possible dangers outdoors should be weighed against the effects on the cat's behavior. While you won't have to put up with daily hunt offerings if your cat is kept indoors, the natural behaviors which your cat will miss out on such as hunting behaviors should be considered. Much will depend on the personality of the individual cat and your circumstances.

So, there's disagreement when it comes to keeping cats indoors: safety versus natural behavior. Owners need to work hard to compensate for the lack of the stimulation if they want an indoor cat and be prepared for the risk if they choose an outdoor cat. Plenty of toys and climbing posts for the indoor cats and be aware of obesity in indoor cats. You can let indoor cats outside, but usually they won't stray very far. Ultimately, no-one can make the decision of which cat to raise but you unfortunately.

Manicure for Cats

Does your kitty disappear when the clippers come out? Do you have to wrap her in a towel to give her a manicure? According to behavior experts, calm, enjoyable nail-trimming sessions are not only possible but that's how they should always be! Check out the following tips for getting kitty to relax while you trim, turning nail-clipping sessions into enjoyable human-feline together time.

Setting the Mood. Ideally you should introduce your cat to nail clipping when she's a kitten. Choose a chair in a quiet room where you can comfortably sit your cat on your lap. Get her when she's relaxed and even sleepy, like in her groggy, after-meal state. Take care that she can't spy any birds, wild animals or action outside nearby windows—and make sure no other pets are around.

Make Friends with the Paw. Gently take one of your cat's paws between your fingers and massage for no longer than the count of three. If your cat pulls her paw away, don't squeeze or pinch, just follow her gesture, keeping in gentle contact. When she's still again, give her pad a little press so that the nail extends out, then release her paw and immediately give her a treat. Do this every other day on a different toe until you've gotten to know all ten.

Get Acquainted with the Clipper. Your cat should be at ease with the sound of the clippers before you attempt to trim her nails. Sit her on your lap, put a piece of uncooked spaghetti into the clippers and hold them near your cat. (If she sniffs the clippers, set a treat on top of them for her to eat.) Next, while massaging one of your cat's toes, gently press her toe pad. When the nail extends, clip the spaghetti with the clippers while still holding your cat's paw gently. Now release her toe and quickly give her a treat.

Never Cut to the Quick. The pink part of a cat's nail, called the quick, is where the nerves and blood vessels are. Do NOT cut this sensitive area. Snip only the white part of the claw. It's better to be cautious and cut less of the nail rather than risk cutting this area. If you do accidentally cut the quick, any bleeding can be stopped with a styptic powder or stick. It's a clever idea to keep it nearby while you trim.

Time to Clip. With your cat in your lap facing away from you, take one of her toes in your hand, massage and press the pad until the nail extends. Check to see how much of a trim her nails need and notice where the quick begins. Now trim only the sharp tip of one nail, release your cat's toe and quickly give her a treat. If your cat didn't notice, clip another nail, but don't trim more than two claws in one sitting until your cat is comfortable. Be sure to reward her with a special treat afterwards. Please note, you may want to do just one paw at a time for the first couple of sessions.

Clipping Schedule. A nail-trimming every ten days to two weeks is a nice routine to settle into. If your cat refuses to let you clip her claws, ask your vet or a groomer for help.

What Not to Do?

- If your cat resists, don't raise your voice or punish her.

- Never attempt a clipping when your cat is agitated or you're upset. And don't rush, you may cut into the quick.

- Don't try to trim all your cat's claws at one time.

- Do NOT de-claw. This surgery involves amputating the end of a cat's toes and is highly discouraged. Instead, trim regularly, provide your cat with appropriate scratching posts and ask your veterinarian about soft plastic covers for your cat's claws.

Overweight Cats

Obesity is an extremely widespread problem in pets and, as with humans, can be detrimental to the health of a cat. The overweight pet has many added stresses upon his body and is at an increased risk of diabetes, liver problems and joint pain. Obesity develops when energy intake exceeds energy requirements. The excess energy is then stored as fat. Once a pet is obese, he may remain obese even after excessive caloric intake stops. Most cases of obesity are related to simple overfeeding coupled with lack of exercise and can be a problem with house cats.

Once the cat becomes an adult, at about one year, feeding once or twice a day is appropriate in most cases. Senior cats, age seven and above, should maintain the same feeding regimen. Once cats reach adulthood, once a day feeding is fine if they are healthy and have no disease problems suggesting a reason to feed differently but you can feed them twice if you like, depending on how active they are.

Many cat owners feed only dry food to their felines. Dry food is fine if it is complete and balanced. Dry food may be less expensive than canned/packaged cat food and may stay fresher longer. Cats that eat only dry food need to be provided with lots of fresh water, especially if they are prone to developing urinary tract blockages. For all cats, constant availability of fresh, clean water is important. Super-sizing food portions is not just a problem for people. Since the feeding instructions on pet food labels are based on the needs of the average cat, you may be feeding more than necessary if your cat's needs are lower than average. If you feed your cat dry food, you may provide it to him at specific mealtimes in measured quantities. Dry food can also be supplemented with a small amount of canned food to make meals more appealing.

Obesity is less common in cats than in dogs. It has been suggested that cats have a much better ability to regulate their own energy intake. Is your cat too fat? As a subjective assessment of body condition, you should be able to feel the backbone and palpate the ribs in an animal of healthy weight. If you cannot feel your pet's ribs without pressing, there is too much fat.

Also, you should see a noticeable "waist" between the back of the rib cage and the hips when looking at your pet from above. Viewed from the side, there should be a "tuck" in the tummy, the abdomen should go up from the bottom of the rib cage to inside the thighs. Cats who fail these simple tests may be overweight. An additional factor to be considered when managing obesity in cats is hunting. It may be necessary to confine your cat to the house to prevent "additions" to the diet.

We recommend that you consult your pet's vet before starting on a weight loss program, but here are some tips for dieting which should include these major areas:

- Correct Diet. Overweight animals consume more calories than they require. Work with your veterinarian to determine your pet's caloric requirements, select a suitable food and calculate how much to feed. The diet should contain a normal level of a moderately fermentable fiber and the type of fat that prevents the skin and coat from deteriorating during weight loss. Diets that dilute calories with high fiber lead to increased stool volumes, frequent urges to defecate and variable decreases in nutrient digestibility.

- Exercise. Increasing physical activity can be a valuable contributor to both weight loss and maintenance. Regular exercise burns more calories, reduces appetite, changes body composition and will increase your pet's resting metabolic rate.

- Owner Behavior Modification. A successful weight management program requires permanent changes in the behaviors that have allowed the pet to become overweight. Perhaps you are giving your pet too many treats, for example, or not giving him enough opportunities to exercise.

If you are committed to your pet's weight loss, here are some important things you can do:

- Remove the pet from the room when the family eats.

- Feed your pet several small meals throughout the day.

- Feed all meals and treats in the pet's bowl only.

- Reduce snacks or treats.

- Provide non-food related attention.

Keeping Your Cat Happy at Home

You may not think of cats as paying much attention when their owners come and go, but some cats can develop separation anxiety when they form a particularly strong bond with their owners. So just as you love and miss the little ball of fur when you leave your cat for work or holiday, it is good to know that your cat misses you too. Keep an eye on your cats for signs of anxiety and take steps to ensure peace of mind in your absence. You have the privilege of taking your phone out and browsing your photos or screensaver of your favorite feline friend, but to my knowledge they don't have mobile phones for cats yet so they don't share the same privilege of looking at their favorite human companion when you leave, so be aware of cat separation anxiety.

Know the signs of separation anxiety. They can range from prolonged vocalizations or excessive grooming when you're away, to urinating on your personal belongings or near the front door or other house-soiling problems (see Beyond the Litter Box chapter for more details on that). Basically, you're looking for anything that's different from their otherwise normal behavior. Make sure your cat's needs are being met. Cats are sensitive to routines, especially mealtime routines. A recent documentary put GoPro recording devices on their cats and it showed that outdoor cats will follow the exact same routine almost every night when they are let out. They will follow the same route like they are patrolling the ramparts of their territorial castle while they keep a watchful eye on invaders, they will visit the same spots and even urinate in the same place every night. They are definitely creatures of habit. For this reason, be as consistent as possible in your feeding habits and daily routines, etc. Also, don't fall behind on litter box scooping despite demands on your schedule. A cat food that helps reduce stool odor might be helpful, too.

Provide opportunities for stimulation. Make sure your cats have plenty of engaging toys to enjoy while you're away. And make the most of playtime when you're available. Playtime limits frustration and helps your cats maintain emotional balance. Check online for tips and pointers on more healthy ways to have fun with your cats or ask your veterinarian to help for ways to cope with separation anxiety issues. If you're still suffering from associated problems and don't see results, your veterinarian may need to take a closer look to rule out underlying health issues or provide additional treatment for anxiety.

Managing Allergies to Cats

You may want to own a cat but you have allergies, are worried about allergies or you may already have a cat and find that your allergies are becoming a problem. The good news is that cats and people with allergies can live together! Phew! There's a lot you can do to make your life easier if you have allergies and a cat. Allergies to cats are caused by a reaction to certain proteins found primarily in secretions from a cat's skin and in a cat's saliva. These proteins stick to your cat's hair and skin and are released into the environment when shedding occurs.

Some people report developing immunity or growing out of the allergy to their cat. While this is certainly possible, don't depend on it. It is also possible that the allergic reaction will get worse with more exposure. If you are getting a new cat and have concerns about allergies, consider a short-haired breed over a long-haired as they release less hair into your home environment. If you are interested in a purebred, consider a Devon or Cornish Rex. These cats lack some of the layers of hair found on other breeds and so may produce less reaction. The Sphinx breed is entirely hairless and extremely affectionate.

Keep in mind that all cats groom themselves and an allergic reaction is caused by saliva just as much as by hair.

Once you have a cat, diligence around the house is key to limiting allergies:

- Wipe down smooth surfaces in the home regularly and vacuum frequently as well

- Frequently wash any bedding that your cat sleeps on

- You may want to restrict your cat's access to certain areas of the house. The allergic person's bedroom is a definite cat no-go zone

- Rooms with hardwood floors will retain less allergens and be easier to clean than carpet

- If you have only a few rooms in your house with carpet, you probably should keep your cat out of those

- Upholstered furniture pieces will retain a lot of allergens so you may choose to keep cats off them or out of rooms that contain them

- Providing the best cat care includes weekly brushing. It will be incredibly helpful in reducing allergic reactions because it helps prevent loose hair from getting into the air. Be particularly careful to groom in the springtime when your cat will be shedding its winter coat.

- Cleaning the litter box regularly will also help because the proteins that cause a reaction in saliva, hair and dander are found in urine as well. Whenever possible, all grooming should be done by someone who isn't allergic to cats. It should also be done outdoors if possible.

You should also talk to your doctor about what anti-allergenic drugs you can take to make your life easier and other possible ways to manage the problem.

Why Do Cats Scratch?

Despite what you may think, scratching and climbing by your cat is not because they are troublesome little things and they like to go out of their way to cause mischief. Cats scratch and climb to leave their scent and visual markings, to sharpen their claws and to stretch their legs. Instead of declawing your cat, provide a scratching post where normal scratching behavior can safely be practiced. Also consider these priorities:

- The right scratching posts. Choose posts that are sturdy and tall enough for your cat to reach up and stretch while scratching. Most cat trees also include scratching areas. Good choices are sisal rope, corrugated cardboard, carpet or wood. Place posts next to areas where your cat likes to sleep. Get a scratching routine started by gently helping your cat do scratching motions and reward immediately.

- Close supervision. Keep watch to prevent climbing and scratching in places other than scratching posts. If scratching or climbing occurs, calmly take your cat to the post to redirect it. Reward or praise your cat for using the post. Consistency is key.

- While you wait for results. Until your cat is using the post regularly, confine your cat to a familiar room with toys, scratching posts, litter box, food and water when you are not able to supervise. Remove any items that may be tempting to scratch. Once your cat is frequently scratching the post, gradually allow freedom in the home without supervision.

- Troubleshooting. Cats love vertical space and will climb on almost anything. If your cat insists on climbing or scratching on your furniture or drapes, have cat trees, cat perches, etc., that are acceptable areas in which your cat can be up high.

Understanding Your Cats Language

A cat's 'meow' is not just a simple cat sound. It's a surprisingly sophisticated method of communication. A cat's vocalization habits and voice are as individual as the voice of a person. You may have a cat that hardly ever makes a peep or you may have one that's extremely talkative. Different breeds will have different sounding meows as well. For example, Siamese cats are famous for their particularly shrill wail.

The most common sort of meow is a plaintive cry for attention. If your cat is walking back and forth in the kitchen, she probably wants cat food and you will probably have noticed the same cry or meow. In cat language, they are probably saying, "please feed me, human". If meowing occurs when you've just come home, your cat is probably glad to see you and wants to be stroked or picked up. The welcome meow, particularly when it is repeated consistently, is also related to mating. A female cat in heat will meow constantly to advertise her availability to males. In some cats, this can develop into prolonged wailing at all hours, day or night.

Sometimes a cat will make strange chattering or even bleating sounds when discovering prey that's unreachable. No one is entirely sure why cats do this. Some suggest that it is simply a sound of feline anticipation or frustration, like someone smacking their lips. Some people even think it's a ploy on the cat's part to get its prey to investigate the strange noise. Growling, spitting, hissing and shrieking are all aggressive or defensive cries. Usually it's clear if a cat is angry or frightened. Similarly, purring needs little explanation. It means your cat is content and happy receiving your love and affection.

It should be noted that if you have a quiet cat that suddenly starts meowing or a loud cat that suddenly stops, it might indicate your cat is sick or unwell. You should pay attention if your cat starts meowing constantly while using the litter box, cleaning herself or eating cat food. Any of these could be signs of distress or some health issues in which you might want to consult your veterinarian.

Your Elderly Cat

Cats begin to show visible age-related changes at about seven to twelve years of age. There are metabolic, immunologic and body composition changes too. Some of these are unavoidable. Others can be managed with diet. Start your cat on a senior diet at about seven years of age. The main objectives in feeding an older cat should be to maintain health and optimum body weight, slow or prevent the development of chronic disease and minimize or improve clinical signs of diseases that may already be present.

As a cat ages, health issues may arise like with any elderly person or animal. Some signs of aging health issues include:

- Deterioration of skin and coat

- Loss of muscle mass

- More frequent intestinal problems

- Arthritis

- Obesity

- Dental problems

- Decreased ability to fight off infection

Routine care for geriatric pets should involve a consistent daily routine and periodic veterinary examinations to assess the presence or progress of chronic disease. Stressful situations and abrupt changes in daily routines should be avoided. If a drastic change must be made to an older pet's routine, try to minimize stress and to implement the change in a gradual manner if possible.

Cat Conclusion

We hope you have enjoyed reading "How to Care for Your Cat: A Complete Guide from Kitten to Adult" and that you have learned everything you need to know including some extra tips and information to take care of your kitty. Cats make great pets and they can be well behaved and very affectionate and loving animals with the right guidance. We hope your time with your feline friend is a long and happy one and you give it all the love and affection that they deserve and that they will reciprocate this love tenfold.

Thanks for reading "How to Care for Your Cat: A Complete Guide from Kitten to Adult".
I hope to see you again soon for some more of our popular pet loving books.

If you enjoyed this book or found it useful, please show your support by leaving a review by clicking on the link below:

First Printing, 2015

ISBN: 9781549515880

Top10 Publishing
123 Oval Road
London, NW1 7EA

Printed in Great Britain
by Amazon

24387570R00027